Memory Makes Us

Poems
by Rich Fernandez

TWO TREES
LIBRARY

Published by Two Trees Library
450 Lexington Avenue, Unit 1187
New York, New York 10163

First Edition: November, 2024

ISBN: 979-8-9906538-0-1 (Paperback)
ISBN: 979-8-9906538-1-8 (eBook)

Published in the United States of America

For the great, unconditional loves in life.

Contents

Memory. 47

Wholeness. 67

Preface

The poems I've gathered here are a series of reflections that span more than three decades of life, from early adulthood to the present. Compiling this book was a joyful journey of rediscovering poems from old journals and notebooks while also capturing new reflections from today. I'm pleased to offer my first book of poetry, a collection of meditations on living and loving in the world.

Nature

The Imaginal

When it comes time
for a caterpillar to transform
into a butterfly

it forms a chrysalis
in which its body dissolves into liquid,
a natural part of the transformation.

This state
is known as
the imaginal.

In it, all possibilities already exist,
the entire coda for what is to become
contained in liquid form.

It may be that for each of us
there is this possibility—
to dissolve away all that
is held so fast and tight

in order that transformation can unfold
and we too can fly free
into the sunshine of a new day.

River's Breath

The mist on the river
in the stillness of the morning
rises gently
in great kindness

moving to greet the world
from which it was born.

This giving of life
a teeming dance
music enveloping all
flowing between the banks
manifest here, now

washing my soul with a clear and
poignant understanding
of dimensions
not knowable but
sensed

just there beyond reach
yet living in my heart
and in the infinitude of my imagination.

Sing river sing
that I may remember
and return.

A Flower Blooms in Its Own Time

What is essential
cannot be rushed.

A flower blooms
in its own time.

The causes and conditions
that allow for this vitality to arise

come and go
as they will

like
the seasons

emerging, abiding and then departing,
ever and always this, just this—

fullness in its own
time and way unfolding

the only way
it could ever be.

52 Names

I visited my friend
who is the head priest
of a very old temple
in Kyoto.

He offered tea and as
we sat and drank he said,
"Did you know that
there are 52 names
for the spring rain
in our language?

"The way it falls
the rate of fall
the different sounds of the rain
when it lands

"each has a name."

He spoke about the
exquisite beauty of
paying such attention
and also about the trap
of giving such defining form
to the formless.

In that place
the 52 names
for the Spring Rain
together with
what has been forgotten

become that narrow gate
through which we pass
to know truth.

Land's End

Here at land's end
there is the song of the tides
and the caress of the sea breeze
everywhere the color of water and play of clouds
the radiance of sun streaming warmly
on a high cliff above the ocean.

In this place
the air is soft
the light forgives
and rhythmic, liquid sound

soothes the ponderous mind
eases the troubled heart
offers without asking
gives without needing

nurturing the spirit
in a kind, gentle
embrace

an invitation to come
and know stillness
a calm abiding
a healing peace

a place where
all that is unconditional
resides

this possibility
to touch into awe
and be renewed.

Sea Jelly

It seems as if the sea jelly
lives a life of great surrender
moving as it does with shifting currents and tides
all seemingly outside any from of volition.

Yet the same sea jelly
sustains itself through the hunt
it's perfectly designed body waiting
and then moving skillfully
when its living food is near.

All of this comprehended when today
a sea jelly washed up on the shore
half buried in the sand
before my feet.

Earlier
it was afloat
in the deep ocean.

So I said a small prayer and offered a blessing
as the sea jelly seemed to have reached
an ending of a cycle, there and then.

I looked away.

Moments later as I turned to leave,
with a last glance
I found that a wave had come
and had taken the sea jelly back out
into the ocean.

Mountain Laurels

In the soft, dappled sunlight of the forest floor
on an afternoon in early June
a chorus

of mountain laurels quietly assembles
bearing witness to the season
and the occasional,

sometimes reverent and
sometimes preoccupied
passersby.

Look closely.

Each stem
of each branch
is erupting
in a whole galaxy of blossoms.

This is an unfolding that
the eye can readily witness—
but in its essence extends
beyond the mind's understanding.

Rather, it is the heart that apprehends it all.

The beauty. The symmetry.
The presence.

The mountain laurels invite
a knowing smile,
a gentle intuition born
of touching into tranquility.

Steel River

Steel river,
you sing to me at night.

Steel river,
your banks are the the city's lights.

Steel river,
I hear your uneasy song.

Steel river,
need I listen to you for long?

Divine Whisper

Out in the wide open spaces
with a plentiful sky and the birds singing
and green everywhere the eyes rest

there is a chance to return
to that quiet, timeless place
at the center of things
where trust is not only possible
but vitally alive.

And all the while a steady breeze arrives
carrying in the cool fog
rolling in almost impossibly over the hills
whispering
of the glory of what is manifest
all around you. And in you. And as you.

Allow yourself these moments
to look, see, and feel
the vastness beyond
the known; any fear; the self.

You and I, we possess
this capacity to be
in every moment of every day
both the seer and the seen.

Komorebi

There is an exact
word in the Japanese language
for when sunlight filters
through the leaves of the trees
in a forest.

Komorebi.

Who saw it
and who named it
and how
is not known.

Perhaps it mattered only
that both the seer and the seen
were ever one always
and the word came
as something in between.

Falling from the Coconut Tree

We watched as the neighbor's
teenage son
climbed up the coconut tree
in the yard of our ancestral home
to harvest the young coconuts
growing there at the top
of the tree in such profusion.

It looked so easy,
his skinny brown arms and legs
shimmying up the smooth tree trunk.

Seeing him, I thought I understood how he did it:
Feet using the little dents
cut into the tree
while his arms hugged the trunk,
limbs moving rhythmically upward in unison.

The way he climbed was easeful,
as if gravity were not a factor.

Eighty feet above ground,
a few well placed swings
of the machete which he had
carried up in his teeth
and the fruits came falling down,
with heavy thuds as they hit the earth.

It all looked so easy
so effortless
that I thought I could do it too.

So the next day
I stood underneath that same tree
and resolutely began my attempt,

grabbing around the trunk
while also trying
to use the footholds.

It took all the strength I had.
It was not easy at all.

Somewhere between steps 3 and 5
I lost my grip
and I fell hard onto my back
slamming into the ground below.

The breath left my lungs and
I blacked out
I thought I might be dying for a moment.

But when my breath came back,
and I took stock of what had just happened
I knew that I was just a silly boy
who had tried doing what other boys
seemed to know how to do
in that place.

But I grew up far from there
in a place where there was snow
not coconut trees
and immediately I knew that I had no business
climbing that tree.

So I stared up the coconut tree
and at the ripening fruits
still clustered there
under the canopy of palm leaves
and I thought, "How beautiful."

The Bay Laurel

The air softens
and an aroma floats in
seemingly coming from everywhere at once
infusing my body
stirring something deep inside
touching all the way down
into my spirit.

The bay laurel evokes memories of life past
and future possibilities
in a infinite field
where everything seems possible
but with quietude.

To the Mountains

In the bright
clear air
you are
met.

The mountains high
and rivers clear
and valleys deep
and sky so wide.

Joined in spirit
trust the call
for it is vibrant
pure and true.

Not bound by
time or space
a deep knowing
living what is given.

Beautiful
mysterious
joyful
blessed.

Bottom Configuration

The way that the waves
take shape
when they meet the shore
is a combination of their long form journey
instantiated thousands of miles away

and the upwelling of rock,
fire or friction born,
a legacy of energies released
now in the form of the unique land mass
sloping or walling up towards a near shore.

Immovable object meeting unstoppable force
then crashing and dissipating
but not without giving life
to whole ecosystems
and organisms

as matter is neither created nor destroyed
but merely changes form.

Love

Sospiro

Raging
I only sought quietude
for myself alone.

But then in your laughing eyes
beneath the sighing trees that day
there was found
a timeless
quiet fire
at the center of things.

No place, no time.
I see you there.

Just a glance and
your scent of flower honey and earth
telling me stories
without words.

Your heart painting a picture
in my mind's eye
which I cannot
remember to forget.

Spring Flower

There along a forest path
the spring flower bloomed
speaking a soft greeting.

I had almost passed
when I heard its whisper,
and I stopped then to witness

jewel-toned blossoms
in quiet, graceful exuberance
declaring:

I am of this world
and subject to its conditions
yet in essence I am limitless and free.

Strong, as I bend with the wind.
Resilient, as I adapt to the seasons.
Vibrant, as I reach always towards the light.

And like all things,
in time
I too will fade and pass.

But for now we are well met
here on this shared path
in the infinity of presence and the eternity of now.

Stay with me then this blessed while,
as we deepen together
into wholeness.

Soon Enough

Eagerly
yearning

struggling against
time and circumstance.

We want it all
now.

Not to be
told
that the path
is long

or worse
that what is desired
will never be.

How to bear
this terrible
burning?

There is but one
way:

To know that
you cannot know,
with great compassion.

So come,
what may.

Exquisite Gravity

A gravity
exists
that calls our
bodies together.

We melt
into
each
other.

The sweet chestnut
aroma of you
the depth of your
kisses

your
curves filling
my hands,
an exquisite invitation

and
your body
opening to mine
in its warm ripeness.

It is said that such
joy is fleeting
but this,
this is timeless.

Entwined
in bliss
nothing short of
transcendent.

All of it
an expression
of our
hearts

and
spirits
which together
sing.

Way Finding

Still after all of these years
I am working to give myself permission
to love.

To hold as primary
what I love
as the source.

To be guided
and held
by love.

To trust
that what I love
is everything I need.

And that it's safe
and true and
first.

Completely

You asked, "what is different about us?"

And I told you, "I love you completely."

Spiritually. Emotionally. Sensually. Intellectually.

It's so easy.

And we make each other laugh.

So that's it.

Everything.

The Prevailing

Once
I thought I
might love
you
but never
gave
it a chance.

Then I lost you
to time
and the winds
of circumstance,

the pull
of convention,
the joys,
and brutalities
of everyday life,

all of
the sacrifices
freely and lovingly
offered
to others.

Then there came
a season
to consider
the important
things

and above all
the people

the
once dear
ones

and the
connections
we shared.

So
I wondered again
about you

and with
a wide smile
and admittedly some
longing
and even
a little
hope

I sought
you out

and found you
again.

You told
me you
were so very
happy
to be
reconnected.

This time
I did not
choose

whether or

not to
love you.

It was much
much
simpler.

Love chose us

with a
suddenness
and profoundness

which made
clear that
everything
needed to
change

and above all
that
never again
will I lose you
to time.

The Promise in Your Kiss

So many secrets are hidden there
on the sweet breath of your kiss

whispering from deep currents
of warmth, devotion and bliss.

A passion abundant
boundless and free

as you join life
in celebration

and your
smile speaks to me.

The quiet strength there
from your sparkling eyes shines

as we drink of passion together
in these uncertain times.

There is solace in these moment
even as we burn to be free

all of it here now
in the way your kiss speaks to me.

Limitless Love

We have argued
about whether unconditional love
exists.

We agreed that
in its essence
the love of a parent for a child is unconditional.

But what about us?
We are lovers, with passion, connection and bliss
and yet we have many conditions that we ask of one another.

"Give me time," I've asked.
"Consider me and and my heart," you have said.

These are needs and conditions we each have,
a conditional kind of love.

"That may be," you say
"but my love for you
is limitless."

That also is true.

So, as for those conditions,
they can be happily met,
in order that we are always able to nurture
the limitless kind of love between us.

Unsaid

Something is spoken
between us
without words
but clearly understood
in the essence of our being.

What was true then
is true now.

You walked in that evening
wide-eyed at this new
life yet
ever curious, open
welcoming.

I was taken
in those first moments
and remain so

now and always.

It is years now of
lives lived and chapters written
of love and heartbreak and hope
so much laughter
so many tears.

And yet what is Unsaid
is still so.

This hidden gem
shining softly
in our depths.

Why or how

we do not know

but we can trust
be grateful and
dream, together.

Your Glance

When you say
yes with your eyes

and then nod your head
with such certainty

I know what you also mean is
"I adore you."

It's no secret
you know.

And I feel the
same.

In such a moment
when you say little

but offer
everything

I rest with you in a place
of timeless peace and joy.

Chosen

Clearly, powerfully
we have been
chosen for
one another.

In the effortless,
easeful weaving of our
hearts, bodies, and minds
together

warmth
passion
laughter
understanding

and also in the
sense of something
much, much greater
still

as when looking
into your eyes
life
looks back and smiles

so it is that
we are called
and welcomed
to that which is eternal.

On Feeling Broken-Hearted Today

It is enough to see the news today
to have the feeling of being broken-hearted.

It is enough to experience the gap
between yourself and those who you love
to have the feeling of being broken-hearted.

It is enough to have tried your best
and to have come up short
to have the feeling of being broken-hearted.

The feeling of being broken-hearted:
an experience
in a field of loving awareness.

Holding this feeling of broken-heartedness
with loving awareness—
that is the invitation,

the practice,
the work of this lifetime,
the gift.

Memory

The Quiet Invitation

In the vividness
of the journey
from being to becoming

amidst the flickering dance
between action and reflection—
alignment emerges.

A close knowing
a path glowing faintly
in the mists of imagination

not so much
chosen
as revealed.

Even as you
stand blinking
in fear or wonder

there comes the still quiet voice
at the center of things
that sweet, gentle calling that whispers:

This is true.
This is good.
This is alive now.

You are called
an invitation to wholeness
in this everyday arc of your life.

Healing Tears

Sometimes there are tears born of suffering
and sometimes tears of joy.

But there are also healing tears

that are rooted both in truth realized
and yet longed for still

such that the tears that come
are both echos of
absence

and songs of
renewal.

Anabasis

The ancient child sings
this softly to
my soul:

Fortune
visits, takes flight,
and returns.

Fear
rears up as a sword
that cuts deeply into the flesh.

Hope
emerges as a star
guiding the way in darkness.

That voice is clear now
and ever more so
with each passing season.

And when I dwell in silence for a while
that song becomes none other than
the voice of experience

reminding me to walk
into the unknown
and find myself in wholeness there.

Memory Makes Us

Where do memories go
when they
disappear?

They must be in you
of you
as you.

No longer so
clear
but felt.

Like your mothers smile
or your father's hand
or an ancestor's spirit.

A worldview is shaped
a way of being embodied
always in relationship
with the people and events
that have inhabited your life.

No matter the remembrance,
memory makes you,
even as it fades.

Sweet Intoxication

Don't you like dying off
just a little bit?

Letting go this experience of
the terrible weight
of living,

un-shouldering the burden

letting it slip into
sweet oblivion
and hoping to find there
the euphoria
that is seemingly absent in the day to day
way of things
and at once entirely, eternally possible.

Sweet intoxication,
arriving in the sometimes subtle,
always seductive
urge to die off,
die off just a litte.

Never Lost

There is an unbroken chain
from your heart to mine
to the next.

Even as memory fades
there is a knowing
etched in us
deeply encoded
in the fibers of our being.

Wake to the realization
that this love so deeply felt

takes form as
a passing

to the next one loved
and the next.

An offering.

In this movement
a legacy lives,
no love lost is ever lost
only ever and always
given.

Seasons, Chapters

Ever changing
the causes and conditions
of our lives,
the context through which we move,

the turning of the seasons,
the many chapters lived,

the people,
the circumstances,
the inner landscape in which
we experience it all.

Triumphs and tragedies come and go,
states of mind and heart,
vitality of spirit.

Feeling exhilarated now,
exhausted then
finding repose and renewal now,
stuckness and pain then.

And always, always there is
the possibility of
beginning again.

Starting with a gentle knowing
that abides at the center of things,
and within you.

An understanding in the form
of an ever present stillness,
a pure and clear source.

These are movements not

seen but felt
quieter than a whisper
yet immediate, intimate.

Such conversations contemplate
an unconditional type of kindness
beginning with your own self

and extending to
those near and far
and the totality of it all.

Seasons turn,
chapters unfold,
and awakening manifests—
a calm abiding,
a loving awareness.

Halo Halo

My mom taught me to eat halo halo,
her favorite treat.

It means "mix mix"
in Tagalog.

Combining,
mixing, remixing

crushed ice, evaporated milk, sweet red beans, ube,
coconut meat, durian, flan, toasted rice, and more.

Complex, rich
as the place -

seven thousand islands of an archipelago
in a warm southern sea.

Cultures, conquests,
the sweep of time all touch in -

Malay, Chinese, Spanish, Japanese and American
came and went and remain,

tribes and customs known,
others lost to memory

and the original inhabitants of the islands
who were small and had black skin.

Halo halo has become a kind of celebration,
a legacy of abundance,

a delicious blend,
tastes and textures,

varied cultures
in one thing

a refreshing
mix mix.

A New Place

There is the smell of promise
when you first enter a new space
that you have chosen to inhabit.

Is it a real thing
or just something in the imagination?

Yet the sense of possibility is almost touchable.

Maybe it's because you know
that memories will form
in this new place

and that for better or for worse
time will pass here
and a different chapter in life will unfold

one to call
your own
all here in this new place.

The Pentacle Flower

Birth
Come alive and share this world
with all you touch.
Awaken with the first, deepest breath
for the fire in your heart burns in all things.

Menarche
And with this world comes laughter
as in the spring there are blossoms.
Hear the song, learn its tune, dance
as the sweet melody infuses the fabric of your soul.

Maturity
One another, one and the same
from this harmony is wrought being.
An ancient dance written on the sands of time
gifted to us in these days of bliss, together.

Menopause
Softly, the many-splendored shapes and hues
fade, are shed, come to rest.
The seeds prepare for the long sleep
whispering to one another
of the dream time.

Death
Take me back to the river source
understanding that what we have sown
are the family that we have loved
the friends that we laughed with
the world that we served.

We embrace the ether
the mystery enfolds us
the cycles turn

and we with them
in grace.

The Texture of Time

There was a song playing
on that perfectly ordinary day
a long while ago
that gave texture to the memory
of that certain time in life.

A quality of feeling
located,
something that can happen to any of us.

But often, we forget
until reminded.

Then we remember as if we
were still there.

Remembering that on such a day there
was a sweetness that was inhabited,
a spontaneous sense
of the goodness of things.

Maybe it was nothing other
than youthful exuberance.

Whatever the case, it happened.
And is there in a memory. And is yet alive.

Every time that song comes on
it's so easy to touch into that experience
as if no time at all has passed.

So for a moment at least,
memory is again alive
as a felt sense, a texture
rooted in and yet apart from time.

The Only Way

The path you walk
in this lifetime
is not your own.

Fate, destiny, design—
you are called to it.

Go with a smile.

Life in and of itself
moves you.

Trust. Surrender. Act.

The world awaits.
The flowering of wisdom, joy and compassion
begins in your own heart and mind.

Awaken, dear one,
as the seeds of peace and freedom
manifest within you.

Signal in the Noise

The only way to distinguish
what is unique

in an otherwise undifferentiated pattern
is to relax

and sit quietly.

Perceive.

Listening with something other
than the conceptual mind.

Understanding is an emergent
property of stillness.

Remembrance

Memory lives in us
as us
taking form each day
in our bodies.

Even as we dance
across vast expanses of
time and space

yet are we found together
in a still place
deep in the heart.

Wholeness

The Feast of Joy

Life is a feast of joy.

Even in sorrow there is the seed of joy.
Look carefully, and you will see.

Find the joy in all you do.

And let what you do also bring you joy.

Sometimes you will have to work for it.

But not too much.

War, and the Beginning Place

We watch in shock, anger and grief as war and devastation unfolds across peoples.

. . .

And there are the families and the children. The families. The children.

. . .

We wonder, "What is to be done?"

. . .

Perhaps the answer is what a beloved monk from another war-torn land once said: "Peace in myself, Peace in the world."

. . .

But when? When? When?

. . .

Maybe not today, because today there is but war.

. . .

But even so today, as a beginning place.

. . .

Even as we watch in shock, anger and grief.

. . .

"Peace in myself, Peace in the world."

. . .

For each one of us.
For the children.
For our world.
For tomorrow.

3:45am

I lay awake
in the stillest part of the night
solitary hours when all is quiet
but for my own mind.

In the darkness I observe
the content and process of thoughts
emotions and sensations proliferating
playing before me
undefinable knowing residing outside of time and place.

Gazing out the window at a rain soaked world
wind whispering
and city lights twinkling—

What of me here wonders on,
ever and ever on
about faces and laughter and passions
worries and fears and maybes
all here at once
in the deep stillness of the night.

I drift.

And when I wake tired perhaps
I look out at the world.
I sigh. I breathe.
The darkness, it pulls.

But for today at least, I look to invite
from someplace close within me
a gentle knowing smile.

Ice Cream Happy

I find that
ice cream actually helps
when things get rough
or because whatever
whenever.

Ice cream provides
a moment of happiness
and bliss
in a flavor of my choosing.

Now you say,
"Well you are just eating
your feelings."

And I would say you are
absolutely right.

To that I would add—
that the ice cream will make me a bit sick
if I eat too much
too often.

But it also makes me happy.

Do you know anyone
who is made unhappy by ice cream?

So while
enjoying this most excellent
ice cream
I am content
being momentarily happy
for now.

The Unlocking

It took all of these years
to loosen convention's grasp
on your mind.

Stories you were told which
tamed your heart.

Beliefs you were taught
which were intended to expand but instead
served to limit your understanding.

You once cherished these conceits
or at the very least clung to them tightly
in the uncertainty of the world.

Perhaps it is because you thought that
they afforded a way
to be in conversation
with what was most essential.

Perhaps they did
in some measure
connect you.

Except when the conversation itself
drowned out the essential,
becoming instead a gray numbing field of noise
in which the clear, pulsing signal was lost.

Looking back now,
you spoke to me of culture
and religion
and perhaps most immediately
about the expectations of family.

All of these meant to connect
you to your own heart.

Yet beneath it all remained the warm questions
which never did and never will go away:
What does the whisper of your own heart say?
What does the fire that burns inside
require of you?

In Solitude

It was only part way
through my day that I realized
I had hardly talked to anyone.

And that the conversation
that seems to have continually been happening
was between me and myself.

Just as well
because I have had
many matters close only
to my own knowing rise up.

And if I had spoken these things to anyone
would they have listened?
And would have it made a difference?

Maybe yes, from a place of empathy,
and I could gain a new perspective
against the quality of my experience.

Maybe yes, I would be less in my head
and more in my body.

Still, time and space have conspired
so that I am to pass these moments
in solitude.

Even whole chapters of time
passed in solitude,

contemplating so many things
that could be shared at best
and at worst drown me
in the noise of ten thousand things.

Or even just one thing in particular that
simply won't go away even if I wish it would.

I bear witness,
in solitude.

Like the fire-colored sunset
I went to look at alone and in silence
for an hour yesterday.

That miracle spoke about all
of the presences and absences
and of how deeply they run.

So it is that this song
emerging from the depths
be it sweet or sorrowful
only I alone can know.

Anxiety

Hello, my most difficult companion.
It is you again.

You came to me again tonight for a visit,
spurring me on to think the worst about tomorrow
and many far away future tomorrows.

You whispered to me
about endless whats
and enticed me to ponder about hows;
you invited me to ceaseless wondering
about sometime whenever
such and such will come to pass.

In your company
I worried myself in ways
unknown even to me.

Where did you arrive from? Why did you come?
And who are you really?

Well, really, there is no you there.
Only me doing this to myself,
not sleeping as the mind
fills with imagined possibilities,
none of them good or happy.

Here is the thing though—almost none of them
will ever come to pass.

Yet in those moments
all imaginings are so potent
that they steal sleep,
my body tenses and braces;
all right there in my warm bed,

in the still, quiet of the night.

It may be that with this
quick and ready mind,
these sharp eyes,
and a warm and open heart,
a fertile ground is formed
for you to take root.

Yet I am not completely consumed.
There is also a quiet path out.
In the breath,
the body,
an invitation to relax one small measure.
A space in which the present moment awareness
is recovered.

And it is in the here and now
a softening happens,
yielding and welcoming
sleep,
arriving as it does with new
and different
dreams.

Some Years

In a single moment of truth
your dreams are spun,
living.

In a single moment of truth
your dreams are shattered,
lost.

Yet
knowing this
you find a way
while you are here

to see some dreams
realized
singing out from your mind, heart and body
into the world

or to recoil when some dreams
are laid waste
nesting irrevocably in your broken heart.

Your spirit lives in this struggle with truth.

Your life is your testimony.
Here is to be found passion,
here pain
and here repose
as you walk the many roads
of your years.

Why, why must it be this way?

Because all experience, and all things
including us

have a beginning, middle and an end
that's just the way of things
and no narrative we tell ourselves,
or argument against it
will change it.

So if things are
as they are,
how might you spend
the years available to you?

Somewhere Along Today

Somewhere along today
the hard thought came:
you are not enough; not adequate; unworthy.

Then the feeling came:
sad; bad; anxious,
a dimming of light and an eroding of hope.

Stop.
Breathe.
Reflect.

You are not your thoughts.
You are not your feelings.
This is just a narrative.

The intricate workings
of a restless mind
and a longing heart.

Stop.
Breathe.
Settle.

Dropping into
kind, loving awareness
gentle compassion

the true state
the basis of the life that you are
your inheritance.

The Gentle Sadness

There are times
when in the air
and in my body
there is a quality of gentle sadness.

I smile sitting in the shade
both the seer and the seen.

Resting here in a deep knowing
a calm abiding
completeness
peace.

Even with
this gentle sadness
I welcome you.

So Fresh, So Clean

It takes about 2 hours
at the laundromat
to wash, dry, and fold
everything.

Oddly satisfying, this necessary ritual.
Everything so fresh, so clean
folded neatly and ready to be
stowed in the designated places
once I get back home.

I had a house for a long time
and we had our own washer and dryer
and doing laundry was different then.

But life changed
and I found myself at the laundromat
along with everyone else
engaging in this necessary ritual,
wash, dry, fold.

It is so comforting somehow.
Calm order, certainty,
accomplishment, it is all
there at the laundromat.

It could be a very different
experience you know.
A sense of being adrift, perhaps,
while at the same time compelled
to the grinding necessity,
the dullness of the mundane.

But it is not like that.
Somehow, it is enjoyable.
Maybe the calm certainty,

order, accomplishment.
So fresh, so clean.

Failing Upward

Sometimes it seems
that certain people can do no harm

no matter the gravity
of what they have done.

Awareness is optional
and perception is variable.

The power of storytelling
is profound for our species.

Stories allows us to aspire and reach the high heights
or bring us low and draw on our most vicious instincts.

This is how to fail upward:
refuse to acknowledge truth.

Tell stories that
turn one against the other.

What happens
when we allow people to fail upward?

Bad things.
Broken things.

But we don't seem to mind.
Or do we?

A Quantum of Kindness

Why is it so difficult
to be gentle
with yourself?

Offering kindness and goodwill
to yourself the way
someone who loves you very much
might do.

Someone who wants
the very best for you.

Someone who would support
you no matter what.

Like a parent or
a sibling or
a grandparent or a certain kind of kinfolk.

Or even as a very good friend
might do
when they stand behind you.

Letting such kindness
be your own, inviting kindness to
take root in your heart and
crystalize in your mind's eye.

Understanding that the gentle words offered
about your current challenges or even the victories
are the very thing that you might not know
to be saying to yourself.

Maybe because you did not hear these words
a long, long time ago when you needed them.

Maybe because what you heard instead was
something mean, which you took to be your own.

Maybe because it has been a long road.
Maybe because you need some rest
or some time to just stop
because everything is so noisy.

So you see,
it is always a good idea
to be gentle with yourself.

Rest easy. You will climb the mountain,
perhaps today, maybe tomorrow
but only, meaningfully,
when you let kindness for yourself
settle in your heart.

About the Author

Rich Fernandez, a writer, teacher, and social entrepreneur, has been a lifelong student of human nature. Rich's fascination with the human spirit sparked his journey to learn from philosophical and spiritual traditions across Asia and Europe at a young age and later to earn a PhD in Psychology from Columbia University. Drawing from this foundation, he founded and led organizations focused on adult learning and development, following years of experience in leadership and organizational development in global companies.

Based in San Francisco, California, Rich is an avid mindfulness and meditation practitioner who finds peace in the tranquility of nature, often enjoying long walks alone or with loved ones. His poetry blends deep reflection with active engagement, encouraging readers to discover beauty and meaning in everyday experiences, human connections, and the natural world.